THE 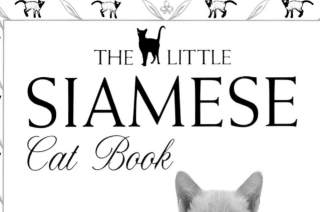 LITTLE
SIAMESE
Cat Book

ELIZABETH MARTYN
DAVID TAYLOR
Photography by Jane Burton

DORLING KINDERSLEY, INC.
New York

A DORLING KINDERSLEY BOOK

PROJECT EDITOR Alison Melvin

ART EDITOR Lee Griffiths

MANAGING EDITOR Krystyna Mayer

MANAGING ART EDITOR Derek Coombes

PRODUCTION Hilary Stephens

First American Edition, 1991
10 9 8 7 6 5 4 3 2 1

Dorling Kindersley, Inc., 232 Madison Avenue
New York, New York 10016

ISBN 1-879431-60-2
Library of Congress Catalog Card Number 91-072733

Reproduced by Colourscan, Singapore
Printed and bound in Hong Kong by Imago

CONTENTS

ORIENTAL
Cat

*The prestigious history
and ancient origins of
the Siamese cat, and its
role in the myth and
folklore of the Orient.*

EASTERN ORIGINS

The earliest known records of Siamese cats date back to the fourteenth century.

No one seems sure where Siamese cats came from originally. Some people say that they were first found in Siam (now Thailand), others believe that this ancient and noble breed of cat originated in China.

FIRST SIAMESE

Siamese cats were not seen in the West until the late nineteenth century when the first cats, named Pho and Mia, were sent to the British Consul General by the King of Siam. The British public caught its first glimpse of Siamese cats at the Crystal Palace Cat Show in London in 1885, where Pho and Mia's kittens were among the prize-winners. The Siamese cat

reached the U.S. several years later, when Lockhaven Siam and Lockhaven Sally Ward were registered in Chicago. But the breed proved delicate at first and the kittens frequently died of feline enteritis until the Oriental cat became better established.

PERFECT POINTS

The original Siamese cats brought out of Thailand were Seal-points, with a characteristic cream-colored coat and seal-brown markings on face, tail, and paws. The first Blue-points, with a bluish tinge to the coat and slate-gray markings, came to England in the 1890s, while the lighter-colored Chocolate-points arrived in about 1900.

Left: 19th-
century
woodblock
of cat
Right:
Japanese
sleeping cat
Below:
Witch cats
of Okabe

Interbreeding between Siamese
of different colors has resulted
in a range of point colors,
including lilac, seal, cream,
tabby, and red.

DARK SIAMESE

The Birman looks like a
longhaired Siamese and,
although it was introduced to
Europe in the 1920s, it was not
granted recognition until the
1960s. The Burmese breed
originated in America in the
1930s from a cat called Wong
Mau, brought from Burma and
crossbred with a Siamese cat.

ORIENTAL LEGEND

Siamese cats are surrounded by myths. Many of these stories concern the sacred cats of the Orient.

In ancient times, Siamese cats had a very important function as guards of the Buddhist temples. Their job was to chase away and even attack thieves who attempted to steal treasure from the temple.

SACRED CATS

The temple cats were regarded as sacred since they were thought to enshrine the souls of the dead. They were kept only by priests and royalty, and anyone caught trying to steal a Siamese cat would be punished by death. No wonder that these cats were unknown in the West for so long. The first Siamese cats, brought to Europe in the 1880s, had squinting eyes and kinked tails, characteristics that have almost completely disappeared as a result of very careful breeding. Elaborate stories were often told to account for some of the early genetic defects in the breed.

ORIENTAL LEGENDS

According to the legend, the Siamese cat developed its squint by gazing so long and hard at the treasure that it guarded. The kink in its tail is said to have come from its habit of curling around the treasure at night to protect it from thieves. Another story relates how a Siamese princess, when bathing, would slip her rings onto her cat's tail, and would kink the end to keep them from being lost or stolen.

*Left: Detail of silk
painting, Cat and
Sparrows
Above: Kitten with
butterfly
Right: Temple guard*

TEMPLE CATS

In Burma, the longhaired
Birman was also kept as a
sacred temple cat. All Birmans
are said to be descended from
one pure white cat, Sinh the
Oracle, who resided in the
Temple of Lao Tsun where the
cats were worshipped as gods.
The story has it that during an
attack on the temple, Sinh

leapt to the defense of his
master, the high priest Mun-
Ha, and was transformed.
Immediately his fur took on a
golden tinge, his amber eyes
turned sapphire-blue and,
where his paws touched the
dying priest, the fur remained
purest white. All Birmans have
kept this coloring ever since as
a result of Sinh's bravery.

HALL OF FELINE FAME

Siamese and Burmese cats have often been the choice of celebrated owners.

The aristocratic appeal of Siamese cats, with their talkative and intelligent personalities, has endeared them to many famous people since the first cats were brought from the Orient in the 1880s.

STAR STATUS

James Mason and his wife were great cat lovers and always had one or more Siamese around the house. Mason liked to sketch the cats, and even wrote a book about them. When he sailed from London to New York, the cats went too. They spent the journey in Mason's stateroom, but suffered badly from seasickness and spent the entire crossing confined to

their basket. Vivien Leigh was also accompanied on a voyage to Europe by her Siamese cat, Poo Jones, who lived with the star in her Hollywood home. The two sailed on the *Queen Elizabeth* to England in 1960, and Poo Jones took a daily stroll around the deck with his mistress. Renowned for his beautiful violet eyes, Poo Jones was a faithful companion who stayed close to Vivien Leigh during her last illness and was by her bedside when she died in 1967.

SIAMESE ON FILM

One Siamese cat who became a film star in his own right was the feline "actor" who played

Left: Prince and Princess Michael of Kent, plus pet Siamese
Above: Milk-drinking Siamese upstages a starlet

Tao in the film of Sheila Burnford's story, *The Incredible Journey*. The Disney film told the story of the intrepid Siamese and two canine companions who trekked 300 miles across the wilds of north-western Canada to find their way home. A couple of unforgettable singing Siamese are featured in the Disney film *Lady and the Tramp*. Their rendering of the song "We Are Siamese" seems to sum up the Siamese personality.

REGAL CONNECTIONS

Siamese cats feel perfectly at home in aristocratic company. Princess Michael of Kent has even issued official portraits of herself accompanied by her Siamese and Burmese cats.

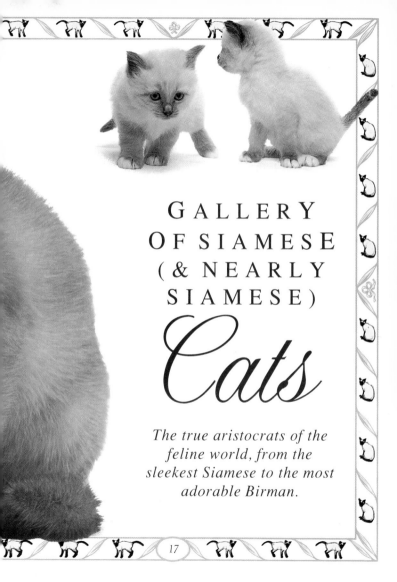

GALLERY
OF SIAMESE
(& NEARLY
SIAMESE)

Cats

The true aristocrats of the feline world, from the sleekest Siamese to the most adorable Birman.

FELINE FEATURES

The Oriental breeding of these pedigree cats shows
in their high cheekboned, wedge-shaped faces.
In longhaired types, the face may be softer and
more rounded. The glorious eyes, most usually forget-
me-not blue, are the most striking feature.

Burmese

Birman

Siamese

Colorpoint Longhair

Snowshoe

Tonkinese

Oriental Shorthair

Balinese

SIAMESE

The best-known breed of pedigree cat, the Siamese is appreciated all over the world. Today's purebred Siamese cat bears little resemblance to the first cats brought out of Thailand in the 1880s. Those Victorian cats had thickset, round heads, squinting eyes, and kinked tails. Systematic breeding, using only the most elegant and fine-boned cats, has eliminated these faults, producing the superb, eye-catching felines that now appear at cat shows. Apart from its obvious visual appeal, the Siamese also has a distinct character; although sometimes a little aloof, it does form a close bond with its owner and is an affectionate pet.

POINTED OUT
The Seal-point is genetically a black cat, but with color appearing only on the points.

CATERISTICS

Oriental, wedge-shaped head with large ears

A loud voice and loads of energy

An extrovert cat with a very strong personality

BLUE-EYED BOY
All types of Siamese have one thing in common: their beguiling blue eyes.

SLENDER BUILD
The Siamese has long, slim legs with delicate paws, on which it moves with deft grace.

COLORPOINT LONGHAIR

This adorable cat brings together the best features of two breeds: the subtle coloring of a Siamese and the strokable, silky fur of a pedigree Longhair. Years of careful crossbreeding between Siamese and Longhairs have been needed to produce the creamy coat with dark points on face, ears, legs, and tail. The Colorpoint is a cat with a lot of character, being more lively than most other Longhairs.

FEATHERY TAIL
The tail is short,
but what it
lacks in length
it makes up for
with soft plumes
of dark fur along
its length. Tufts of
fur on the toes are
another of this
cat's characteristics.

CATERISTICS

Saucer-like eyes in brightest sapphire

Luxurious, silky fur

Gentle and loving, but with plenty of Siamese spirit

SELECTIVE BREEDING
Colorpoint Longhairs are bred in many different colors. The Seal Tabby-point is one of the most recent varieties to be recognized.

LUXURIOUS COAT
Although this cat has the markings of a shorthaired Siamese, its body shape is inherited from a Longhair. It is sturdy and stocky, with short legs and a round, wide face; full, fluffy cheeks, and a short, almost snubbed, nose.

BURMESE

Although related to the Siamese, Burmese cats have glossy coats of a uniform color, with no distinctive point markings. The body shape is different too, being more muscular and heavier than that of the Siamese. The hind legs are a little shorter than the forelegs, while the face, although wedge-shaped, is more rounded and not as elongated as that of the Siamese. The Burmese is less vocal than its close relative, but it shares the same love of people. It is a sociable breed and is easy-going and tolerant with children, making it an excellent and affectionate family pet.

BROWN BEAUTY
The satin-like coat shows off the rich sable-brown color to perfection. Brown was the original coat color of the Burmese. The breed was first introduced from Burma to San Francisco in the 1930s, as a "dark Siamese."

CATERISTICS

Fond of people; likes plenty of company

High sheen on the fur, which is dense and short

Slightly slanting eyes of glistening gold

BRIGHT EYES

All Burmese have arresting golden eyes, the clearer and brighter the better.

LUSCIOUS LILAC

The creamy coloring of the Lilac Burmese is thoroughly appealing.

BIRMAN

In a class of its own, the Birman has markings rather like those of a Siamese, but all four paws are white. On the hind feet, these white "mittens" should extend up the back of the legs in a series of pointed spurs. One great attraction of the Birman is its easy-care coat which, although of medium length, does not mat and requires only light brushing to keep it immaculate.

SACRED CATS
The Birman became a recognized breed in the United States in 1967. It is sometimes known as the "holy" or "sacred" cat because of its origins around the temples of Burma.

CATERISTICS

White mittens
on all four feet

Adapts well to
other animals

Coat does not
need much
grooming

LIVELY CHARACTER

The Birman has a longer
body and narrower face
than most other
longhaired cats,
although it is not as
lithe as a Siamese.
It has a lively
and bold
personality.

BLUE EYES, DARK FACE

Vibrant blue eyes set in a
soft, dark face make a
stunning effect. The
eyes are round, with a
slight upward slant at
the outer corners. The
coat is fine and soft.

Snowshoe

The Snowshoe breed was developed in the United States and is something of a rarity. It originated from three white-pawed kittens, born to Siamese parents. These were used to start a breeding program and, once the type was established, American Bicolored Shorthair cats were used to develop it further. The cat has point markings and a short, glossy coat like a Siamese, and the dainty white paws that are typical of a Birman.

Noble Features
This aristocratic breed of cat has a noble face with high cheekbones, slanting blue eyes, and wide-set ears.

Silver Mittens
The Blue-point Snowshoe has a creamy white body with paler chest and abdomen and dark grayish-blue points. The cat is also bred as a Seal-point, which has a medium-brown body, darker points, and white paws.

SLEEK SILHOUETTE
The Snowshoe is a medium-sized cat, bigger and heavier than the Siamese, but with a lithe and athletic body. Its fur is sleek with a good, glossy shine.

CATERISTICS
Pure white paws

Sparkling blue eyes

Not high-strung;
loves being shown

TONKINESE

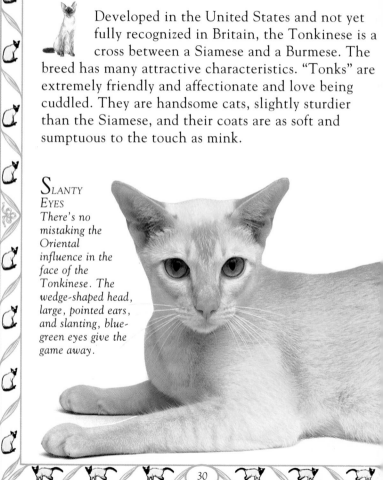

Developed in the United States and not yet fully recognized in Britain, the Tonkinese is a cross between a Siamese and a Burmese. The breed has many attractive characteristics. "Tonks" are extremely friendly and affectionate and love being cuddled. They are handsome cats, slightly sturdier than the Siamese, and their coats are as soft and sumptuous to the touch as mink.

Slanty Eyes
There's no mistaking the Oriental influence in the face of the Tonkinese. The wedge-shaped head, large, pointed ears, and slanting, blue-green eyes give the game away.

CATERISTICS

Pleasant, outgoing
character. Very fond
of people

Fur has a natural
sheen and feels just
like mink

Long, tapering tail

PUREBRED "TONKS"

Tonkinese can present a problem for
breeders, because when two similar
Tonkinese are mated, only half the
resulting litter of kittens is likely to be
true to the breed.

COLOR VARIETIES

The Red-point Tonkinese was first
bred in Britain. The colors of the coat
take several months to
develop fully.

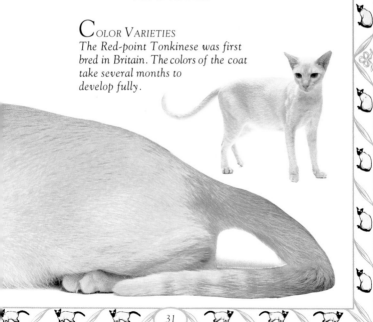

31

FOREIGN SHORTHAIR

The Foreign or Oriental Shorthair, in all its myriad variations, is the result of breeding Siamese cats with other shorthaired cats. This cat has a uniform coat color with no point markings, but it has all the elegance and distinction of the Siamese-type body and face, as well as its endearing and lively personality. The breed was recognized in the late 1970s and there are more than 30 color varieties, ranging from black, white, and red to tabby and tortoiseshell.

ELEGANT PROFILE
The Foreign Blue boasts a coat of dark gray with a distinct bluish tinge. A sleek, svelte creature, it has ultra-fine, smooth-textured fur that lies very flat. The body is lithe and slim with long, slender legs, and is offset by a lean tail that tapers down to a fine point.

EMERALD GREEN EYES
Foreign Shorthairs differ from Siamese, not only in their lack of points, but also in the color of their eyes. Most varieties have vivid green eyes, although for some color types, eyes of amber, dark orange, copper, or sapphire-blue are permissible.

ORIENTAL TABBY

This is no common or garden tabby, but an Oriental Chocolate Tabby Shorthair. The typical tabby swirls and stripes show up to perfection on its athletic body. The pointed face and large ears indicate its Siamese blood.

CATERISTICS

Much like the Siamese in shape

Alert and curious

People-lovers that make good pets

BALINESE

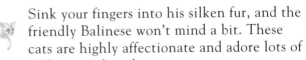

Sink your fingers into his silken fur, and the friendly Balinese won't mind a bit. These cats are highly affectionate and adore lots of attention. They are thought to have originated as a longhaired variation of the Siamese, and are now bred in their own right. They have the same markings and lean body shape as the Siamese, but have slightly less extrovert personalities. With their glamorous looks and loving natures, they make perfect feline companions.

BIG SOFTY

The Balinese coat is delightfully soft and strokable. The fur is shorter than that of most types of longhaired cat and may even have a slight wave.

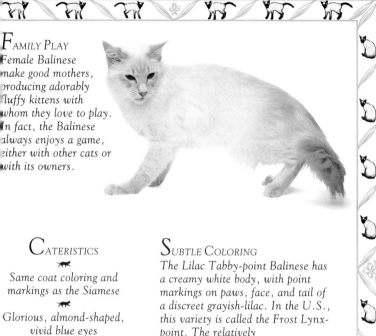

FAMILY PLAY

Female Balinese
make good mothers,
producing adorably
fluffy kittens with
whom they love to play.
In fact, the Balinese
always enjoys a game,
either with other cats or
with its owners.

CATERISTICS

🐈

*Same coat coloring and
markings as the Siamese*

🐈

*Glorious, almond-shaped,
vivid blue eyes*

🐈

*A charming personality
that loves people*

SUBTLE COLORING

The Lilac Tabby-point Balinese has
a creamy white body, with point
markings on paws, face, and tail of
a discreet grayish-lilac. In the U.S.,
this variety is called the Frost Lynx-
point. The relatively
tangle-free coat
benefits from
grooming
every day.

INSCRUTABLE
Cat

*A guide to the Siamese
temperament: choosing a
name, cat psychology, and
feline birth signs.*

NAMES AND NAMING

"The Naming of Cats is a difficult matter," wrote T.S. Eliot in *Old Possum's Book of Practical Cats*. He didn't make it any easier by suggesting that cats should have "three different names": one "the family use daily," one that's "more dignified," and one known only to the cat, a "deep and inscrutable, singular Name." Here are some suggestions specially chosen to suit a cat of Oriental origin.

ASIA *The continent that gave birth to the Siamese cat.*

CAPPUCCINO *For a creamy white Seal-point Siamese cat with markings of darkest, richest coffee.*

CORIANDER *A fragrant herb, much used in Thai cookery.*

CRYSTAL *After the nineteenth-century Crystal Palace Cat Show where the Siamese cat was first seen in public.*

GALANGAL *A ginger-like spice, common in Thailand, and used to give fire and flavour to many dishes.*

JEMMA *One of the first Siamese to be exported. Jemma was a male, but Gemma would be a suitable female name.*

LAPIS *The brilliant blue gemstone, lapis lazuli, has the same intense color as the eyes of a Siamese cat.*

PAVAROTTI *For a Siamese who likes to exercise his vocal cords loudly, melodiously, and in front of an admiring audience.*

PYEWACKET *A Siamese witches' cat, who was featured in the play Bell, Book and Candle by John van Druten.*

RAJAH *The original Burmese cats who guarded Buddhist temples in Burma in the fifteenth century were known as Rajahs.*

RANGOON *Capital of Burma, a city full of exotic atmosphere.*

RUSSELL *After Major Gordon Russell, recipient of a pair of Birmans given to him by Tibetan priests in 1919.*

SUNNY *For a cat who thinks the whole world revolves around him.*

SUSIE *Short for Susie Wong, the beautiful half-Burmese character in Paul Osborn's play of the same name.*

TSUN *In honor of Tsun Kyan-kse, the blue-eyed Burmese goddess whose temple was patrolled by Birman cats.*

Understanding Your Siamese

Does your cat have any difficult personality quirks that you find hard to handle? Here are the knottier parts of the Siamese psyche, unraveled.

Attention on Demand

My two-year-old Siamese, Wong, expects immediate attention whenever he demands it. He yowls for food and cuddles, and shouts even louder if he wants to go in or out. And if we don't obey instantly, he sprays us.

🐈 Wong is obviously a particularly clever Siamese, and has worked out exactly how to get his own way. One glance at his quivering tail-tip has you running to pander to his whims, rather than face the consequences. What you have to do is get the upper hand by ignoring Wong's demands and giving him attention when it suits you. You'll have to put up with his furious spraying for a day or two, but fortunately this cat is clever enough to learn a new pattern of behavior once he realizes that his old tricks don't work any more.

Scaredy Cat

Thistledown is my affectionate Birman who has suddenly become terrified of strangers. When the doorbell rings, she hides under the bed and won't come out until the coast is clear.

🐈 Has Thistledown been scared by a noisy or insensitive guest recently? If so, she is probably obeying her survival instinct in avoiding any new threat. To regain her confidence, put her into her carrying case, and place it in the room where you entertain guests before they arrive so she can't run away. To reassure her, visitors should come into the room accompanied by someone familiar to Thistledown. Ask strangers not to approach the cat, but to sit down

quietly some distance from the basket. Repeat this procedure whenever you have guests, and gradually Thistledown will learn that visitors do not pose a threat. However, it may be some time before she completely gets over her fear.

Hypersensitive

Maisie, my Siamese, adores being stroked – except on her abdomen. If I tickle her there, she often bites and leaps out of my arms.

🐈 Cats seem to be able to go into a state of blissful, baby-like relaxation when they are being stroked and cuddled, but many cats dislike being touched on their sensitive abdomen and hind legs. Then they suddenly feel vulnerable and trapped, and respond with their best self-defense mechanism – their teeth and claws. The simple answer is to avoid stroking your cat's more ticklish areas.

Deep Thinker

All cats have their foibles – Siamese more than most.

Cat Birth Signs

Find out all about your cat's Chinese birth sign.

The Sign of the Goat

*February 15, 1991 – February 3, 1992
& January 28, 1979 – February 15, 1980*

The Goat is a sign of great charm
and cats born under its influence
will endear themselves to their
owners and everyone they meet.
Although shy at heart, these cats sparkle in front of an audience.

The Sign of the Horse

*February 27, 1990 – February 14, 1991
& February 7, 1978 – January 27, 1979*

Suave and elegant, cats born in
the year of the Horse are highly
aristocratic creatures. Intelligent
and quick learners, these cats love
being the centre of attention, and are sometimes very excitable.

The Sign of the Snake

*February 6, 1989 – January 26, 1990
& February 18, 1977 – February 6, 1978*

Snake cats are renowned for their
grace and good looks. They have a
tendency to indulge in frantic
bursts of activity, but there is also
a more reserved side to their character. Solitary by nature, they
spend long hours sitting quietly and thinking by themselves.

THE SIGN OF THE DRAGON

February 17, 1988 – February 5, 1989
& January 31, 1976 – February 17, 1977

Highly intelligent, Dragon cats
are quick to seize opportunities
and never miss a trick. Born lucky,
they are outgoing and energetic
felines. Cats of this sign are often arrogant and flamboyant.

THE SIGN OF THE CAT

January 29, 1987 – February 16, 1988

What soothing companions these
cats are. They are often home-
loving, and warmth and comfort
are vital to their happiness. Well-
mannered, they take particular
pride over their appearance and are always beautifully groomed.

THE SIGN OF THE TIGER

February 9, 1986 – January 28, 1987

Impulsive and brave, cats born
under this lucky sign tend to act
first and think later, which can
get them into trouble. The owner
of a Tiger cat needs to be very
watchful, as these energetic and extroverted creatures love
exploring and their adventurous spirit leads them far from home.

THE SIGN OF THE BUFFALO

February 20, 1985 – February 8, 1986

This sign can be inscrutable in the best Siamese tradition. Although they may sometimes appear aloof, Buffalo cats are shy and often wary of strangers. It is impossible to read their thoughts and they won't encourage you to try.

THE SIGN OF THE RAT

February 2, 1984 – February 19, 1985

If anything interesting is going on, a cat born under the sign of the Rat will be in the midst of it. Curious and gregarious, these cats usually lead eventful lives. They adore their owners and will do almost anything to please them.

THE SIGN OF THE PIG

February 13, 1983 – February 1, 1984

Extremely vocal, with a wide repertoire of sounds, cats born under the sign of the Pig make sure that they are understood. Peacemakers, who hate the sound of arguments, they will intervene to try to cool heated tempers. They are lovers of luxury and have expensive tastes in food.

The Sign of the Dog

January 25, 1982 – February 12, 1983

Alert and interested, cats born under this sign will follow you around everywhere to see what you are doing. They tend to dislike being left alone and prefer human company. Moodiness can be a problem with these felines.

The Sign of the Rooster

February 5, 1981 – January 24, 1982

Rooster cats are very volatile and sometimes behave impetuously. The rest of the time they wear a dignified air and stroll around, tail erect, with great pride. Although they are devoted to their owners, they can be very self-centered.

The Sign of the Monkey

February 16, 1980 – February 4, 1981

It's easy to be taken in by the Monkey cat's delightful personality, but cats born under this sign can be devious. They are clever at getting themselves out of tight corners and know how to assume an air of innocence. These cats are easily bored, perhaps because they are so intelligent.

PAMPERED
Cat

*All the devoted owner
needs to know about the
care and pampering of
Siamese cats.*

CHOOSING A KITTEN

It can be so hard to decide which is the kitten
for you, that you'll want them all.

PURE WHITE KITTENS

Siamese kittens are
often smaller at birth
than other breeds. When
born, the kittens are pure
white. The gene that
produces the "points" on the
face, paws, and tail is
sensitive to heat and the
markings appear gradually
on the cooler parts of the
body. Although kittens
are usually born blind,
the sapphire-blue eyes of
the Siamese are sometimes
half-open when the kittens
are born, and open fully
shortly afterward.

SHOW KITTENS

*If you plan to show your cat, buy
from a reputable breeder and ask for
full documentation of the pedigree.*

WHICH KITTEN?

When you visit a litter to make your choice, watch the kittens at play for a while.

1 Choose one that is pert and lively, with lots of energy and an inquisitive nature.

2 Make sure that the kitten runs and jumps easily.

3 Look for bright eyes and clean nose and ears.

4 Open the mouth and check that the teeth and gums are sound and healthy.

5 Look through the fur for any signs of fleas.

6 Siamese cats adore human companionship, so don't choose one unless you can return the love that your pet will give.

KEEPING WARM

When you take your kitten home, let him settle in completely before allowing him to explore outside.

LITTER MATES

Two kittens are twice as much fun as one, and will be happy companions.

CAT GLAMOUR

Most Siamese-type cats have short hair, which makes grooming straightforward. However, if you own a longhaired variety such as a Colorpoint or Balinese, you will need to groom your pet every day to prevent the thick coat from becoming tangled or matted.

No More Tangles
Longhaired cats should be gently brushed and combed every day.

Tips for Grooming

1 Rub grooming powder into the coat, making sure that it is evenly distributed.

2 Brush through the fur, dealing with any tangles that you come across.

FELINE FACIALS

Clean the outer ears gently with a cotton swab and wipe carefully around the eyes with a damp cotton ball.

TOOTH CARE

The teeth can be cleaned to prevent a build-up of tartar. Use a soft toothbrush with either a solution of salt water or feline toothpaste available from pet shops.

3 Finish with an all-over brush, using long, sweeping strokes down the whole body.

4 For extra gloss, rub the coat gently with a piece of velvet, silk, or chamois.

EXOTIC CUISINE

Although cats should not be given highly spiced food,
many of them do enjoy well-flavored dishes. Here are
some gastronomic goodies guaranteed to tempt the
most selective feline appetite on those special days
when you want to lavish a little extra affection on
your cat. Allow food to cool before serving.

Chicken Stir Fry

*Dice raw chicken breast. Heat
oil in a wok or frying pan and
cook the meat quickly over a
high flame, stirring all of the
time. When the chicken is
almost cooked, stir in a few
flaked almonds for added
crunch. Allow to cool
and serve with a
little plain
boiled rice.*

Aromatic Fish

*Place fillets of flounder or scro
in a foil parcel. Pour over a littl
milk, season, and sprinkle wit
finely chopped coriander. Bak
in the oven for 20 minutes o
a medium heat. When cooked
flake, remove any bones, an
serve with the cookin
liquid poured over
Garnish wit
coriander*

Shrimp Temptation

Mix cooked shrimp with plain
yogurt and pile onto squares of
toasted whole grain bread.

Oeuf Royale

Lightly scramble an egg beaten
with a tablespoon of milk, and
stir in slivers of smoked salmon.

Steak Tartare

Fresh steak or hamburger, very
finely ground and served raw,
will make your cat's eyes light
up. Raw meat should only be
given as an occasional treat.

Chicken Liver Risotto

Cook chopped chicken liver for
about ten minutes in a well-
flavored stock. Stir into plain
boiled rice and sprinkle with
chopped mint or parsley.

Salmon Delight

Remove the bones from
canned salmon
and mix with
cooked pasta.
Sprinkle
cheese on
the top and
melt under
the grill. Cool
before serving.

Fresh Fruit Parfait

Siamese cats are often
partial to fresh
fruit. For this
dessert, put
two table-
spoons of
plain yogurt
in a bowl. Top
with tangerine
or slices of apple.

My Cat's Personal Record

Name ....

Pedigree name ....

Sex ....

Date of birth ....

Breed ....

Color of eyes ....

Description of markings ....

Name and breed of mother ....

....

Name and breed of father ....

....

Name and address of breeder ....

....

....

Cat show prizes ....

....

Foods favored ....

Foods frowned on ....

Favorite drink ....

Best possible treat ....

Vocabulary (list sounds and meanings) ....

....

....

Body language (describe movements and meanings) ......

....

....

Attention-seeking ploys ....

....

Cat tricks and games ....

....

Most precarious perch ....

Preferred snoozing places ....

Special stroking zones ....

....

A-Z OF SIAMESE CATS

A IS FOR AFFECTIONATE
Siamese cats often form a devoted attachment to those who care for them.

B IS FOR BREEDING
If you want to breed pedigree kittens from your Siamese cat, consult a professional breeder. A Siamese crossed with a non-Siamese can also produce beautiful and very sturdy kittens.

C IS FOR COAT
The close, smooth coat benefits from daily combing, which removes any dead hairs and keeps the fur immaculate.

D IS FOR DELICATE
Although it is a myth that Siamese are a delicate breed, they do love comfort and need a warm basket and plenty of good food.

E IS FOR ELEGANCE
Long, slender legs and a very svelte bodyline give the Siamese an elegant look.

F IS FOR FOREIGN SHORTHAIR
The name given to a shorthaired cat bred from a Siamese crossed with other types. Foreign Shorthairs come in a wide variety of different colors.

G IS FOR GENES
In the past, careless breeding has produced weak kittens with faded markings. Stricter control has resolved the problem.

H IS FOR HEAT
There's no mistaking a female Siamese in heat. The breed is renowned for its strident mating calls and restless behavior, which can go on for several days at a time.

IS FOR INTELLIGENCE
Many Siamese cats are exceptionally bright and can solve problems with considerable skill and dexterity. They are sometimes willing to learn tricks, although they will usually only perform when it suits them. Some city owners have even managed to train their Siamese cats to walk on a leash.

IS FOR JEALOUSY
Perhaps because a Siamese becomes so attached to his owner, he also tends to resent the intrusion of other pets and, sometimes, other humans. However, if introduced when very young, Siamese cats can become good friends with other animals.

K IS FOR KITTENS
Although small at birth, Siamese kittens soon develop a healthy appetite. Start them on solids when they are about four weeks old.

L IS FOR LOSING
Nothing is more distressing than the loss of a much-loved pet. Never let your cat stay out all night because this is when accidents tend to happen. Give an early evening meal to lure night-loving cats indoors. Once inside, shut the cat flap firmly.

M IS FOR MOTHERHOOD
Although Siamese cats do make excellent and loving mothers, they sometimes need help at the time of the birth. For some reason, the breed doesn't always know how to deal with newborn kittens. Consult your vet about this if your cat is about to produce a litter. The vet should also be notified of the likely date of the kittens' arrival so that he can be on hand in case there are complications.

N IS FOR NEUTERING

Unless you are planning to show or breed from your cat, it is kindest to have him or her neutered at between four and six months old.

O IS FOR OLD AGE

Fifteen or sixteen years is a good average age for a Siamese. An older cat will eat less and sleep more than a younger animal and will appreciate a warm bed in a draft-free spot.

P IS FOR POINTS

The name given to the typical Siamese markings on face, paws, and tail. There are lots of possible colors, including seal, lilac, tabby, blue, and cream.

Q IS FOR QUICK WITS

The canny Siamese is always quick to spot an opportunity for extra food or a comfy bed. They are also good at outwitting their owners and are extremely clever at getting into places where they shouldn't be.

R IS FOR REGISTRATION

Registering the details of name, color, and parents is a must for pedigree kittens, and should be done when they are around five weeks old. Register all kittens with a cat registry, who must also be notified about any change of ownership. Take advice on this from your breeder.

S IS FOR SHOWING

The attention-loving Siamese has a good temperament for showing. On the day of the show, the cat must be healthy, perfectly groomed, and allowed plenty of time to settle down in his cage before judging. Get your pet used to being handled by strangers before the show to avoid any sign of nervousness during judging.

T IS FOR TEETH

Brush teeth gently with a soft toothbrush and salt-water solution to prevent a build-up of damaging tartar. The breath should be pleasant and the gums firm and pink. If you suspect a rotten or painful tooth, take your cat to the vet for its extraction.

U IS FOR UNDERSTANDING

A Siamese cat is happiest when he has plenty of human companionship and love. He will quickly feel neglected if left alone for long periods, and will go to great lengths to recapture your full attention. Treat your Siamese cat with plenty of care, and he will be your devoted friend for life.

V IS FOR VOICE

One outstanding characteristic of a Siamese is its voice, which is quite unlike that of any other cat. These cats often enjoy "talking" to their owners, answering with a whole range of sounds. Siamese cats can be demanding and their loud howls for attention cannot be ignored for long.

W IS FOR WATER

Don't worry if your Siamese turns up his impeccable nose at a bowl of fresh water and refuses to drink. Cats extract a lot of liquid from their food and can manage on hardly any water without harm. Make sure that clean water is always available though, just in case your cat suddenly develops a thirst.

X IS FOR XTROVERT

This is not the breed for the cat owner who is looking for a placid pet who sleeps all day by the fire. A Siamese loves nothing more than an admiring audience. Your extrovert pet will keep you entertained with his antics, acrobatics, and mischief.

Y IS FOR YOGURT

A healthy addition to a feline diet. Offer a little of the plain variety for your cat to sample.

Z IS FOR ZEN

An Oriental method of contemplating the inner nature in order to achieve enlightenment.

I N D E X

ACKNOWLEDGMENTS

Key: t=top; b=bottom; c=center; l=left; r=right

All photography by Jane Burton except for:
Animals Unlimited: 40–41
The Bridgeman Art Library: 10, 11t, 13
Camera Press (photo by Norman Parkinson): 14
E.T. Archive: 11b
Ronald Grant Collection: 15
Images Colour Library: 12
Dave King: 9tr, 17tr, 18tr, 19tr, 19c, 19b, 22–23, 26–27, 28–29, 30b, 31b,
32–33, 34–35, 47tr, 50–51

Design Assistance: Patrizio Semproni, Rachel Griffin, Camilla Fox
Additional Picture Research: Diana Morris
Illustrations: Susan Robertson, Stephen Lings, Clive Spong